WHEN THE AFFAIR IS OVER

Untold Stories from the Other Woman

BOOK ONE

GILLIAN'S STORY

WHEN THE AFFAIR IS OVER

Untold Stories from the Other Woman

By K'Trie

WHEN THE AFFAIR IS OVER: UNTOLD STORIES FROM THE OTHER WOMAN

COPYRIGHT © 2019 K'TRIE

ALL RIGHTS RESERVED. THIS BOOK MAY NOT BE REPRODUCED IN WHOLE OR IN PART BY ANY PROCESS WITHOUT WRITTEN PERMISSION FROM THE COPYRIGHT HOLDER.

CERTAIN NAMES HAVE BEEN CHANGED OR OMITTED TO PROTECT THE WOMEN WHO ARE SO DARINGLY SHARING THEIR STORIES.

ISBN: 9781695180055

INTERIOR BOOK DESIGN BY K'TRIE

COVER DESIGN BY K'TRIE

PUBLISHED BY K'TRIE

PRINTED BY KINDLE DIRECT PUBLISHING

DEDICATION

DEDICATED TO THOSE WHO ARE WORKING TOWARDS MOVING BEYOND THEIR PASTS.

Preface

This is **HER** story. Each of these stories will depict the other woman's perspective, not as a victim, but as a woman who exercised bad judgment and lost sight of herself. Society has always pointed fingers at the other woman, the notorious side chick as the culprit of broken relationships, where cheating was involved. A negative spotlight has followed those women who have fallen in situations where morals were superseded by feelings and overshadowed by empty promises. She is not without fault, but she is not the only one to blame. She was the one HE ran to, confided in, when his life was in disarray. What he thought he was not getting at home, he looked for in her. She was his dirty, little secret. She is not a victim, but she is a pawn in a dangerous game that she never imagined she would play. What society fails to realize is that the other woman carries the guilt of the affair, even after it's over. She is not out to hurt anyone, most of the time she is not even the initiator of the affair. Even if she was, he still did not say NO. When the affair is over, the other woman is left with pieces of broken promises. When the affair is over, and HE has moved on, the other woman faces the sheer reality that she was just a fix, a temporary habit for HIM to escape his reality of commitment. The woman, formerly known as the side chick must now move on, hoping to regain her self-respect and dignity.

WHEN SHE FIRST MET HIM

    Gillian was a talented, attractive, intelligent, and independent woman moving up in the world. She was a recent college graduate trying to get her foot into the professional environment. After months of looking for a job, she had finally found something in her field. She felt blessed and was excited to start this new venture. Gillian remembered this was the day she met HIM. When she met HIM, she could see a seductive look in his eye, unaware that she was being marked as potential prey for his deceitful game. Although, she noticed this look, she quickly brushed it off. "Maybe he is just very friendly", she thought. Gillian's first impression of HIM was innocent, she saw him as only a coworker. She did find him attractive, but she was not the type to chase guys, well not anymore. Based on her previous experiences and the mindset that she now acquired, the last thing on her mind was hooking up with anyone. After the last heartbreak, Gillian was focusing on her career, she was trying to find her happy place again. She was in a place where she held onto her principles and worth, call it learning from the harsh lessons from the past. Repercussions from giving too much to the wrong people enabled her to find a fresh new beginning for herself. However, little did she know that the mistakes that she thought were in her past would soon be revisited......

LETTING HER GUARD DOWN

As Gillian became acclimated to her new job, she noticed the different personalities in the office. Some people she considered as friends, some she chose to keep at a distance. Gillian's personality made her somewhat of a threat, because she was friendly, but sometimes people misconstrued it as flirtatious. Gillian was an attractive woman and it caught attention. Sometimes the attention made her uncomfortable, but she didn't pay it any mind. The initial attraction between Gillian and HIM did exist, he was handsome, charming, and he seemed like an all-around good person. Gillian didn't mind conversating with him, he made her laugh. He was a breath of fresh air in a strenuous work environment. Their conversations started out as innocent, just general or work-related issues. Then, as Gillian let her guard down, he became a real, good friend.

Gillian assumed he was a single man by the demeanor he exhibited. However, she discovered that he was married, which didn't bother her, because she wasn't trying to get with him. Yes, she was attracted to him, but that was it. The friendship with HIM continued, and Gillian noticed how he would try to sneak certain sexual comments towards her into conversations. Some of these comments went over her head and others she simply laughed off. Gillian knew how to change the subject before a conversation went off the deep end. But like any woman, Gillian began to have thoughts that made her rethink whether she should continue conversing with HIM. Nonetheless, Gillian was not one to judge him, whatever he did behind closed doors really didn't concern her. She considered him a friend and at that point, that's what she needed. Gillian continued falling for his friendly act and was unaware that this was the beginning of something that would one day change her from the inside out. Unbeknownst to Gillian, she was now a pawn in his game, she was now at a vulnerable state where she was easy prey.

    Months passed, the conversations got longer. Her intentions were innocent, however, others perceived her as a seductress, trying to get HIM into her sensuous web. Gillian in no way wanted to get involved with a married man. "Who wants that drama", she asked herself. He was flirtations with her, but she knew the limits. When this flirtation occurred, she would quickly divert the conversation. Gillian began to find herself backing off from talking to HIM and observed his interactions with other females. Gillian noticed his flirtatiousness with other females and began to wonder if he was really the faithful man he said himself to be. Regardless of his indiscretions, Gillian was focused on achieving her goals and being a topic of the rumor mill wasn't one of them.

LETTING HIM IN

Gillian remembered the day he asked for her number. Despite her reservations, she gave it to him, thinking it was okay since they were friends. This trust placed her in position for his true ulterior motive. Phone conversations were few, but they would text each other. If she wasn't at work, he would text to check in on her and vice versa. Thinking back, Gillian recalled one phone conversation in which one statement should have been the signal for her to avoid him. The statement he made stated his true intentions and Gillian just laughed it off, not knowing how serious he was. Maybe she was naïve, or just oblivious to the fact this married man was trying to pursue her.

The day IT happened would forever stay in Gillian's mind. That day was a pretty good day, it was Friday, the weekend was coming, and Gillian was so glad that she was off that following Monday. That meant extra rest for her. That evening after work, Gillian received a phone call from HIM, he wanted to know what she was doing. Gillian was chilling at home; she was enjoying some free time. "Can I come over, what's your address", was the next question she heard. Gillian remembered that she replied with a questionable "Sure", then gave him the address. In the moments she spent waiting for HIM to come, Gillian's conscience was going back and forth, reassuring herself that nothing was going to happen.

Gillian had been abstinent for a few years, and she was not going to fall into a trap of temptation. She then decided to retract the invitation. But before she could pick up the phone to tell him no, the doorbell rang. Gillian walked nervously to the door and there he stood there with a big, toothy grin on his face. That evening, they sat and talked about different things, it was innocent. He turned on some music and they danced, Gillian was a little uneasy when he got a little too close to her. She could smell his cologne and she felt her body grow warm as he held her close.

When the music ended, she was determined she was going to ask him to leave, then he kissed her. His kiss ignited her whole body, making her pull in closer, and succumb to temptation. As he rubbed her body, every curve, her inhibitions disappeared. Gillian felt as if the air hit triple digits as he stroked her breasts, taking time to fondle each nipple. She felt every inch of his manhood pressing against her as his lips sucked and bit the hot spot on her neck that drove her wild. Gillian's mind was saying no, but the loud moans from her body drowned out her conscience. She was too lost in the ecstasy. When he entered her body, the freaky part that lay dormant within her was awakened. It was wrong, but the sex felt so right. The morning after, reality set in. Gillian never thought she'd be in this situation. She had always tried to do the right thing. She lay in bed thinking how she just laid aside her morals for a night of passion. She had made a promise to herself that she would never be used again. She had never slept with a married man. She realized this was the start of something she couldn't come back from.

LETTING HIM STAY

    After that night, Gillian felt like she has lost all her worth. All the standards she had set for herself disappeared in that one night. During the next following days, she tried to tell herself it was all a crazy dream, never again will it happen. But he became a habit she couldn't shake, it was as if he knew what to say. He knew where to touch her. She lost herself in him. But it wasn't just about the sex, the talks they had behind closed doors would be about his home life and other things. He would always say, "I would never hurt you" after Gillian would talk about her experiences.

    Gillian found herself unknowingly falling for him. He portrayed boyfriend-like tendencies, but Gillian knew he would never leave his wife. He would get upset at Gillian when calls and texts went unanswered questioning why she didn't respond. He would pop by unannounced on days his wife was unavailable, making sure to cover his moves with his homeboys. This secret was eating Gillian up, and his gestures to her in front of others was going to tell it all. Gillian didn't know what to think or do. She knew it needed to end, but how was the question. As the affair approached a year, the sneaking and creeping began to lose their excitement. Faking orgasms became a norm. Maybe it was the sex that lost its luster or Gillian's conscience was finally setting in. But the feelings that Gillian was developing for this man, this unavailable man would not go away. She became the type of woman she never wanted to become, the obsessive type. Gillian found herself texting him all the time, receiving no response. Tears filled Gillian's eyes as she thought about how stupid she was.

A WOMAN SCORNED

Throughout her life, Gillian had made so many mistakes, but this struck her to the core. Her morals, her principles were compromised. She recalled the looks, the comments, and wondered how stupid she was to ignore the signs. Guilt and shame clouded her mind as she tried to cope with the things she had done. Sleepless nights brought about images Gillian wished she could delete. She began to hate herself. Friends and loved ones saw a change in her, they saw the once smiling woman now holding a sadness in which they didn't know the source. "I am okay" was a response that Gillian had programmed for those who expressed concern. Gillian began to work on her aspirations hoping idle thoughts would eventually just wither away. She began thinking that staying busy would eliminate the hurt, but she was wrong. It wasn't fair that she was still feeling this way. She was carrying the guilt of two people, while he enjoyed the lifestyle of a convenient marriage. She didn't know what she wanted from him.

Gillian's mind began to wonder if his wife knew what a dog he was. The signs were clear, how would she not see that this man was disrespecting her. Maybe she didn't care. Gillian's anger became a devil on her shoulder telling her to air out his dirty laundry. Her anger kept telling her that he didn't care about her feelings, so she shouldn't care about his. He chose to step out on his marriage. He chose to pursue her. Gillian was single, she didn't make any vows. She wasn't the type to sleep around but if she did, then that was her prerogative. But she gave that special part of herself to him foolishly. Just the thought of that made Gillian's heart burn with feelings of vengeance. Gillian found herself on his wife's social media page and scrolled to her contact information. Her manicured fingernail tapped the left button on the mouse, as she sat back and pondered if this was the right thing to do. She wanted to come off as someone looking for peace, instead of a bitter ex-side chick. However, she wasn't bitter, she was angry and hurt, and she was tired of feeling that way.

    As she began to type her message, Gillian could feel tears falling down her face, pain that hid deep within poured into her words. She wanted his wife to know everything. Reading through what she had typed, she saw her hurt and anger reflected through her words. In her words, she saw flashbacks of the sleepless nights she cried over how he dismissed her. Her words told a story of shame that no woman should ever have to go through. Gillian felt her pressure rise as she stared at the send button. "All it takes is one click, and she knows everything", Gillian thought. Closing the page without sending the message, Gillian wondered how she would let this go. For so long, she was holding on to the hope that she would get some closure. But the closure she needed was within and it started with forgiving herself.

LETTING THE AFFAIR GO

Gillian pulled out a piece of paper and decided to write a letter to herself. In the letter, she encouraged herself to let all the pain go. She told herself to not feel guilty and ashamed any longer. Tears fell upon the paper as she reassured herself that she would be okay. In her heart, she knew that God would move her past this. This was not the first storm she encountered, and it wouldn't be her last. In the letter, Gillian told herself to find that love for herself, because she was special, talented and beautiful, and to not let anyone or anything turn her heart cold. The love she needed would come when she least expected it.

As she wrote her letter, she thought about how much she wanted her mom right now. She envisioned her comforting smile, but Gillian felt her mom was looking down on her in disappointment. The thought of her mom's disappointment brought a tear to her eye. She also thought about how if her father found out about what his little girl did. She could imagine the look of disappointment that would fill his face. She knew her father loved her nonetheless. But when asked how and why this happened, Gillian would have no response, she didn't know herself. It was all a mistake. After she finished her letter, she held it close to her heart and began to pray for peace and healing. Lord knows, this was something that would never happen again, it couldn't happen again. She made a bad choice and its repercussions made her question her sanity. Not only did this affair test her heart, but it showed her she needed a stronger spirit of discernment. In the end, Gillian wanted to move on and look back on the affair as a learning experience, one she would never forget.

DROPPING THE VICTIM STATUS

In the aftershock of the affair, Gillian first considered herself a victim, but her soul searching led her to a state of acceptance. Through her healing process, Gillian accepted her responsibility in the affair. She knew better and like her father always said if you know better you do better. Gillian's conscience took her to a time when all the signs pointed to his intentions, it took her to where she questioned some of his actions but chose to ignore what was clearly in sight. However, in this situation, Gillian wanted to deflect the heartbreak and place all the blame on HIM. The fact was she wasn't a victim, she was a participant, and it was time she owned up to that. Gillian realized that a huge majority of the anger she felt was at herself for making such a stupid decision. She knew he was married, therefore, all the blame wasn't on him. This wasn't the first time. Gillian thought back over the years and found that most of the heartache she had experienced was the result of her trusting nature.

The quick trust she instilled in others caused her to have high expectations and when those expectations turned out disappointing, she ended up hurt. Her over-trusting nature produced a haze that clouded her judgment when it came to those of the opposite sex. This haze intensified when physical intimacy became involved. Physical intimacy filled a small void of what Gillian was looking for, but it still left a huge hole in her heart. She wanted more, she needed more, she was worth more. Someday she wanted to be a wife, a mother. If she kept on the same path, allowing herself to be used for the sexual gratification of others, she knew that heartache and shame would be a continuing cycle in her life. Sex did not keep a man, it alone wouldn't make a man love her.

  Gillian knew she offered more, but she settled for less than her worth. Time had passed since she made the mistake of sleeping with HIM. The anger and hurt that Gillian had experienced was like a bad memory. Each time his name was mentioned, she closed her eyes, and the rage that once controlled her made a guest appearance. She remembered the angry words that she expressed to him, receiving no response. She remembered trolling his and the wife's social media pages, wondering if his wife finally wised up and left his ass. Gillian looked back on all the time she wasted harboring anger that was ignored. However, this was all in the past. It was time for focus and the time she spent focusing on a bad situation was not going to help her spirit. Gillian needed peace, not closure. Her spirit had been wounded, because she did the unthinkable, she went against her own morals. Determined to drop the victim status, Gillian started a new journey.... a journey to finding herself.

FINDING HERSELF AGAIN...

The journey of self-discipline and soul-searching provided a cleansing of Gillian's soul. This period of cleansing would allow Gillian to focus on herself, who she was and who she aspired to be. During this journey, she would gain discernment. This period of cleansing was to open her eyes so that she could see things more clearly, especially when it came to matters of the heart. Gillian was determined to guard her heart during this journey so that she could understand and know what she needed more than what she wanted. She wanted God to prepare her for her true purpose. She knew that God would move her past that place of pain and allow her to love herself again, so that true love would find her when it was time. God knew the shame Gillian felt, he saw the tears she cried, and he saw the guilt eating at her, but all this was a prerequisite to her journey. All this was necessary and provided the motivation for her to better herself.

On this journey, Gillian had a checklist of goals she wanted to achieve but had put on the backburner because of self-doubt. As Gillian began to mark off her personal checklist, people saw a change in Gillian, a happier version that was no longer controlled by hurt and anger. Gillian saw a change in herself every time she looked in the mirror. She saw a new woman who was more confident. Her confidence exuded from the inside out and the light that was once dimmed within her shone bright. Gillian found herself fulfilling goals she never imagined. Talents that once lay dormant came to the forefront as encouragement for others, but as an outlet for herself. Her creativity was ignited to venture into different avenues that benefited both herself and others. There were still remnants of past regrets present, but they longer had a hold on her. She found herself smiling more, learning to encourage others, including herself. Gillian thought about the lesson in everything and the pain she once wished on HIM, but she didn't anymore. With a new peace of mind, Gillian saw the past as nothing but a footstool to a better future.

A NEW CHAPTER??

Gillian's journey allowed her to grow more and more as a person. Many of her aspirations became realities and she was happy again. Her confidence and self-esteem were at a new level. She now appreciated herself and recognized her worth. The mistakes of the past no longer harbored over her, the fruits of temptation no longer seduced her, because she had developed self-control. Her focus was still on the checklist she had set for herself. During her journey of self-discovery, temptation tried to veer her off track. Temptation brought about guys who started off genuine, but eventually revealed all they wanted was a good time in the sheets. Gillian had fallen into like a couple of times, but her standards had evolved, if sex was the only goal, then she wasn't interested. Meeting guy after guy with the same mentality led to her putting a wall up around her heart.

After finally mastering the art of guarding her heart, Gillian felt that she could open her heart again. Her journey from a broken heart had taught her to discern between lust, like, and love. So, she thought. That's when she saw him. Although, they only glanced at each other, he seemed familiar, like she knew him. This sense of familiarity caused her to reach out. She was never the type of woman who pursued a man, but she had to take a chance. She sent him a friendly message through social media, hoping to break the ice. She found out he had noticed her in the past. He knew more about her than she thought, and the conversation was a breath of fresh air. This guy was young, captivating, sort of handsome. She found out he was also a pastor. By him being a minister, he had an air of confidence about him. This confidence is what mostly attracted Gillian. Because of his position and presence in the church and community, Gillian assumed that he wasn't like the other guys she encountered. She thought that he might be good for her, the type of man she needed in her life. This assumption would eventually repeat to Gillian a valuable lesson, to never judge a book by its cover.

RELIVING THE CYCLE

    Conversations were friendly at first, he would say things that made her smile. He seemed interested in all the things she was involved in. Despite the wall around her heart, she saw a real potential with him. This was the first guy in a long time she began to like. In a short time, the conversations, on his end went from PG to rated R. This should have been the point where Gillian should have exited. Still, the conversations continued, sparking Gillian's inner sexuality. She could talk a good freaky game, because she knew what she could do, but that didn't mean she was going to give it up. Gillian found herself with the same high expectations from this guy like the others. But she was so into this guy, that even the obvious red flags were ignored. Her interest overshadowed the fact that they only talked through social media, he never asked for her number.

    Her infatuation for him allowed her to settle for bullshit responses to questions about going out. He would pacify her with responses such as be patient or enjoy the journey. Gillian wasn't one to rush things, but she wanted to know where this was going, if it was going anywhere. Although Gillian's interest in him remained innocent, it became obvious he was just like others she had encountered. He made it evident that all he wanted was a booty call, someone who stroked his ego and manhood behind closed doors. A relationship or commitment was nowhere on his mind. Gillian was just an option, a woman among a pool of other women he showed interest in. He wanted a personal freak in private, while he played the role of an upright pastor in public. Gillian now knew his position meant nothing. Gillian also dubbed him the "Penis Pastor", not only because he acted like one but because he also sent unsolicited pics of it to her. Speaking her mind didn't mean anything to him, and she found herself repeating the cycle of apologizing for how she felt, even if she was speaking the truth. Maybe he thought Gillian was needy, but he never wanted to understand what was bothering her. Why would he, when he had a whole circle of people who enabled his inflated ego. Gillian didn't want to relive this cycle, becoming infatuated with someone who wasn't into her, only to end up hurt. Yet, the cycle seemed to start again…….

PLAYING THE FOOL AGAIN

Succumbing to the inner demons that plagued her spirit, Gillian found herself in a disturbing, recognizable place. In the past, she had occasionally compared herself to other women, neglecting to appreciate who she was, her looks, her successes, etc. Here she was again, now wondering what she was lacking and comparing herself to the women that this man publicly entertained and flirted with on social media. What was he looking for? Was she not good enough? Was she not pretty or successful enough? Self-doubt clouded her mind causing her self-confidence to plummet to a familiar low level. In the mirror, she saw a shell of a woman, one whose once-reignited inner glow had once again been extinguished by the rejection and disregard of a man she foolishly allowed into her heart.

Gillian found herself becoming mean, depressed, crying to herself, forcing a smile to hide the hurt within. But despite how hard she tried to hide it, others could see her hurting. She was disappointed again, but the only silver lining was that Gillian's intuition had warned her to keep her treasure chest under lock and key, it warned her not to open her legs for this fool. Not only did Gillian's intuition play a major part in her preventing the same mistakes again, but God's divine intervention was present. In those times, when she almost succumbed to the charms of HIM, God intervened, so that she didn't make a bad decision. Although it stung to develop feelings of interest, Gillian realized that this guy wasn't for her, because he had the same motives as other HIMs before, and she had to let go. She knew regardless of how much she cared about him, there was no potential in whatever thing was. In other words, it wasn't going anywhere.

    His ego was so elevated, nothing fazed him. Plus, there were too many unknowns. Gillian didn't really know anything about him, and he wasn't too gung-ho about volunteering any critical details that she needed to know. One of these unknowns was of his true relationship status. The question of whether he was married, divorced, seeing someone was always hanging around the edge of Gillian's mind. Gillian was bold enough to ask him if someone was already in the picture, because being a side chick again was out of the question. "Hell, no, not again", she thought to herself. Although he told her no, something still didn't sit right with Gillian. In addition, Gillian saw his thirstiness exhibited through some of his actions. She saw the women he constantly flirted with on social media. Gillian soon perceived him as an attention-seeker, perpetrator, and not to mention a want-to-be playboy. He craved others' approval, which boosted his arrogance to a disgusting level. This type of man was all too familiar to Gillian, and not in a good way.

TRUTH IS A BITTER PILL

  Gillian began to hate him. To his congregation and others, he was this soul-stirring, great, motivating pastor, but to Gillian, he was a self-righteous, egotistical human being. She put a lot of stock into his position, expecting him to have higher standards. However, this misplaced trust minimized her learning who the true individual was first and foremost. Gillian allowed him to manipulate her into thinking she was the problem. He stated she was the reason he decided to not pursue anything further. Maybe her headstrong or no BS attitude was off-putting to him. Maybe he didn't know how to handle a strong woman. Gillian had always been headstrong and independent, it was how she protected herself, as well as her heart. He didn't know her story. He would've learned that, if he really wanted to know her. Or maybe it was because he didn't get what he wanted, which was between her legs.

  Gillian always had a strength about her, but her strength had now diminished. Caring for someone who didn't care about her seemed to drain her. Her reality felt like a cloudy haze in which she just went through the motions. He never wanted to know her, what made her tick, what made her happy, he was all about himself. Gillian wasn't perfect by any means, but neither was he. The only difference was he hid behind a pulpit spouting scriptures, gathering amen after amen for his approval collection. Yet, he was living foul. Her grandmother used to say rumors were no longer rumors if everybody is saying the same thing. At the end of the day, she realized he was just a man. He was just a man who like many others before used Gillian's good heart as ammunition to make her start doubting herself, her worth. In his mind, he didn't think he did anything wrong. This hurt Gillian to the core. His conceited attitude about the situation told Gillian what she needed to know. The bitter truth was he just didn't care, never did. Friends she confided in had tried to tell her this before, warning her of what kind of reputation he had. They warned her that she expected too much of him. Gillian could now see through the sheer persona he put on as if he was a good, upstanding man. The veil was no longer over her eyes. Now, Gillian felt stupid, like a fool. A negative scar was once again left on Gillian's heart, and it meant nothing to him. Gillian could talk till she was blue in the face, but for what, he still had an amen corner to bolster his arrogant personality. Her feelings and opinions didn't matter to him.

HELLO, FURY

In the beginning, Gillian had her pre-misconceptions about him, but she never judged him, despite what she heard. She liked the person he was in the beginning of it all, that is until his true self made an appearance. It was obvious he judged her, especially after her reactions upon seeing his true colors. Gillian's hate for him increased, wanting him to burn. Confusion and anxiety overtook Gillian as she lost sight of the queen she was. No matter how hard she meditated and prayed, the only thing she wanted was for him to hurt like she hurt. His indiscretions were hidden, but he didn't realize he had awakened a beast within Gillian. Rage overflooded her heart awakening a fury that she had kept dormant for so long. Her kind-heartedness had been taken for granted, and she was enraged. Every sincere word he ever said, now held the label of bullshit. Messages that showed an inkling of concern were just part of a script, one where he told Gillian what he thought she wanted to hear. The way he dismissed things was wrong and the residual anger left in Gillian's heart would not let her have peace. Gillian knew she wasn't the first, and she wasn't the last, but she needed to get past this and move on, by any means necessary.

She knew conversations with him were not one-sided. Gillian could overreact and overanalyze sometimes. True, some of Gillian's actions were less than honorable or ladylike, but they were reactions to his inconsideration to her feelings. However, Gillian was not afraid to live her truth even if some details portrayed her in a negative light. She wasn't scared to own up to her shit. Unlike him, Gillian's reputation was built on being true to who she was rather than seeking approval, putting on a front. Rather than acknowledging his wrong or stating his true intentions, he diverted everything on her. She was portrayed as the only villain in this sordid tale. This in turn caused Gillian to retaliate, letting her anger and disappointment control her thoughts, therefore affecting the words from her mouth. From experience, she knew words hurt, but her heart was hurting. She didn't know what to say or do anymore, she just didn't want to care about him or his feelings. Gillian started to treat him like he treated her, which included her coming out of her respectful nature and mocking him and his ministry. It wasn't intentional, but Gillian was heartbroken.

Revenge wasn't Gillian's forte, but she was tired of the same repetitive bullshit. She was sick of meeting guys with the same catch-the-coochie mentality. He could walk around all day long as if he had no faults, but it was all an elaborate act. Gillian realized exposing him would give the perception of a bitter woman, but how many other women were victims of his manipulative games? How many other women did he seduce with the same script? How many other women did he skin and grin at with false intentions? How many other women assumed his position held standards only to find out it was just a title? How many other women ended up feeling the same exact way Gillian was feeling now, but were scared to express it? When was his day of reckoning coming? When was karma going to deal with him?

RE-EVALUATION TIME

    The whole ordeal with this man left Gillian asking herself why she always attracted this type of man, the arrogant species. What kind of vibes was she putting out? The inner workings of her mind started to wonder if real love was even possible for her. Why did she seem to always attract guys who were unavailable, meaning attached? She even started to question if she was even a good person. Even after the rejection and realization, Gillian found herself reliving some behaviors of the past. Gillian knew this man wasn't for her, she knew he didn't want her, yet she still cared about him. In her innermost mind, she would have thoughts that somehow, she met him for a reason. But reality dealt a heavy blow, when someone truly wanted you, they showed it, they made you feel special. This man made her feel worthless, when she was a prize. This man showed her someone she didn't need, but she couldn't see it. She still opened like a book, exposing feelings and thoughts only to be shot down.

    Gillian found herself going to his social media often, with no reason at all. She knew he had probably moved on to someone else, as all manipulative people usually do. She was angry that he led her on, but the saving grace was that she preserved her virtue. She was grateful that her journey of self-discovery had allowed her to establish self-control as it related to physical intimacy. Her self-discipline throughout the past few years allowed for clarity, even though she was hurting inside. However, Gillian's sanity was tested, she would flood his inbox, trying to communicate with him. Gillian's hope for closure included a hope that perhaps they could become something. However, these hopes were shattered as she realized he was never going to change for himself, especially, not for her. Why was she so consumed by this? She thought she could get her point across to him. She thought they could have a mature conversation. It became obvious he was too into himself to have a civil conversation with Gillian. His interest in a mature conversation only resided within a circle of those who told him what he wanted to hear. He would never realize the extent of how he damaged people with his narcissism, his holier than thou attitude.

    His self-absorbed inconsideration pissed Gillian off. Her spirit was bruised. Here she was, foolishly trying to make amends, trying to bridge the gap between her and this self-centered fool. Gillian was one who always believed in reconciliation. She had once thought that the bridge between HIM and her could be repaired, but she now realized it could not. It didn't matter anymore, she had finally come to terms with what it was. Not even a friendship with him served no purpose in her life. Why was she intent on trying to get him to see things from her point of view? She was beginning to feel like a broken record playing the same song over and over. Why was she still holding on to false hope? It was as if her mind and heart couldn't get in agreement. Her mind was telling her to let it go, but her heart was holding on.

    Gillian remembered her level of confidence and happiness before she reached out to him, a decision she now regretted. Before taking that step, Gillian was centered, but now trust and self-esteem issues reared their ugly heads again. Loneliness was setting in, even as life was going well for her. Gillian wished there was a delete button to remove the thought of him, of all the wounds of her heart, all the things that disrupted her path to peace, to healing. This hurt like hell, because Gillian thought she was beyond this stage. Instead, this was a step backwards. Yes, she had seen the red flags beforehand. She should have learned who he really was before she liked him. She should have left the situation before her heart got in it. She felt like she was going crazy. She loved herself, but not who she became when it came to him. Maybe she did seek attention, so did he. But to him, her feelings were a joke, every time she spoke her mind, it meant nothing to him. Gillian's inner demons played on her self-esteem. In her heart, she wanted to move on, but her inner rage wanted to unmask him, show the world who he really was. Gillian knew that wasn't her, but it wasn't fair. She was tired of being disrespected, reduced to, and being assumed as a whore, as someone quick to give it up to any and everybody. That's not who she was, even if it was a small part of her past. She was worthy to be truly loved, by a man who truly accepted who she was, flaws and all. In return, that love would be reciprocated back to him, and he would be treated like a king. She was worthy to be wanted by someone who didn't want just physical intimacy, but someone who wanted a deeper connection. She was worthy of a man who wanted to know who she was and interested in everything that entailed her world. She was worthy of a king, who not only saw her outside beauty, but someone who saw her for the queen she was, both inside and out. She was worthy of someone who thought she was worth it.

QUEEN, FIX YOUR CROWN AND STRUT

    Gillian had always been a giver, a supporter for both her family and friends. It was in her DNA to love hard, to care hard. Her charismatic and overly-friendly nature was a blessing and a curse. Perhaps heartbreak from losses of the past had confused her heart to a point where she didn't know how to express herself the right way. Maybe she sometimes pushed people away. The negative things that plagued her mind almost distracted her from the positive things in her life. There were too many goals that were near-completion. She was so blessed, but the haze left by him, the false interpretation of love produced by herself, distorted her view. Gillian knew that she had to get it together. She remembered the promise she made to herself years ago. She had vowed to be cautious with her heart, to not fall so easy, to guard her heart. This promise had been broken. Depression and anxiety now invaded her spirt. Why was she stressing about this lowlife? She was stronger, she was better than this. God had given her abilities and gifts that inspired and motivated others. These gifts should have helped her encourage herself, but Gillian knew she needed to get herself together before she self-destructed. She now understood she had to work on herself first. She began to work on herself spiritually, shifting the focus to her goals, and regaining her peace. She needed to get her life back again. This meant getting her, mental, physical, and emotional issues in balance.

She remembered the last time she ran into HIM. He had an uneasy disposition about himself, which was a surprise to her. How is it that the one who hurt and judged her so harshly felt uncomfortable in her presence? Her disdain for him temporarily turned to pity. She knew she had insecurities, but so did he, even though he put on a façade for the world, to maintain his image. Maybe this heartache was a blessing, because Gillian was able to see his soul and it alarmed her. Sitting a few feet from her was someone who preached values, forgiveness and respect, but had no remorse for his wrongdoings. He held no regret for the residual damage that he left upon Gillian and maybe other women, who foolishly became interested in him, who fell for his act. Those who flocked to him, grasped his teachings would never hold him accountable or call him out, even for the things they knew about him. With so many telling him what he wanted to hear, it was obvious he would never acknowledge his errors, when he was in the wrong. Gillian knew that only God could make him answer for everything. Only God could change him, make him a better man. One day God would hold him accountable. For Gillian knew that it was only God who could bring her through this hurt, make her whole again, in the end, making her a better woman.

      Gillian knew she would never receive an apology and she was content with that. "The truth is a hard pill to swallow", Gillian thought. But she knew who HE was now, a charming liar. Maybe God wanted her to see him for what he really was and for that Gillian was grateful. She was also thankful that God allowed her to take inventory within herself, reevaluate who she was and who she aspired to be. Her longing for companionship made her lose sight of that. Perhaps this chapter was needed to realign her focus, as well as give her a new spiritual outlook. Gillian still had residual feelings for him, but she knew that they would go away one day, because they sprung from futile conversations with HIM. There was nothing to keep holding on to because they weren't ever in a real relationship. The truth was that her ability to love, to open her heart had been shaken. The loyalty that she should have saved for someone true had been given to someone with false intentions. Her heart was broken, but she knew she would be okay as time moved on. Gillian would no longer continue to grieve the demise of something that never was. True, genuine love would come, she just had to be patient and love herself first. This was just another storm, and like others she would get through it. She knew her breakthrough and healing were on the horizon. She had to trust God's timing.

Gillian recognized her worth and who she was. In the end, that was all that mattered. "Never the fool again", Gillian said as she held her head high. Tears fell from her eyes as she prayed for God to guide her through this, to allow her to finally let go, to forgive herself first, then eventually forgive him. She prayed that karma wouldn't be as unkind to HIM as he had been to her. Gillian wanted to wish him the best, but she couldn't. Maybe one day. She wasn't bitter; however, she knew her self-care was of top priority. Before she could genuinely forgive those who wronged her, she had to come to terms with herself. In her mind, she bid all the negative memories goodbye. Gillian realized there was a lesson in everything she had experienced in her life, from the loss of those she loved dear to heartache, both past and present. These experiences and feelings showed her what she needed to see, adding to her inner strength. What she was feeling now wasn't about how the pastor or the other men from her past treated her, it was about what she allowed. No longer would anyone make her question her self-worth. No longer would she settle for anything or anyone that did not add happiness or peace to her life. No longer would she forget who she was, especially whose she was, a queen, a child of the Most

High. With this new mindset, she believed a brighter day was coming soon………when she would finally be free of the past. Gillian smiled to herself as a wave of relief enveloped her. She felt a flame burn within her; her faith was slowly reigniting. As she sighed a deep breath of hope …. she claimed today as the start of a new story, one where Gillian finally embraced and loved who she was, who God made her to be. It was time to live her purpose. It was time to wear her crown proudly. In this new story, she would learn from the lessons of her past and live happily ever after………

Made in the USA
Monee, IL
01 January 2024